OUR ANDROMEDA

BOOKS BY BRENDA SHAUGHNESSY

Our Andromeda

Human Dark with Sugar

Interior with Sudden Joy

BRENDA SHAUGHNESSY

OUR ANDROMEDA

COPPER CANYON PRESS

PORT TOWNSEND, WASHINGTON

Printed in the United States of America

Cover art: Rebecca Horne, *Untitled,* 2010

Copper Canyon Press is in residence at Fort Worden State Park in
Port Townsend, Washington, under the auspices of Centrum. Centrum
is a gathering place for artists and creative thinkers from around the
world, students of all ages and backgrounds, and audiences seeking
extraordinary cultural enrichment.

LIBRARY OF CONGRESS CATALOGING-IN-PUBLICATION DATA

Shaughnessy, Brenda, 1970–
  Our Andromeda / Brenda Shaughnessy.
     p. cm.
  ISBN 978-1-55659-410-6 (alk. paper)
  I. Title.

PS3569.H353097 2012
811'.54—dc23

                              2012021010

98765432 first printing

COPPER CANYON PRESS
Post Office Box 271
Port Townsend, Washington 98368
www.coppercanyonpress.org

for Cal

CONTENTS

3. ARCANA

4. FAMILY TRIP

OUR ANDROMEDA

I. LIQUID FLESH

ARTLESS

is my heart. A stranger
berry there never was,
tartless.

Gone sour in the sun,
in the sunroom or moonroof,
roofless.

No poetry. Plain. No
fresh, special recipe
to bless.

All I've ever made
with these hands
and life, less

substance, more rind.
Mostly rim and trim,
meatless

but making much smoke
in the old smokehouse,
no less.

Fatted from the day,
overripe and even
toxic at eve. Nonetheless,

in the end, if you must
know, if I must bend,
waistless,

to that excruciation.
No marvel, no harvest
left me speechless,

yet I find myself
somehow with heart,
aloneless.

With heart,
fighting fire with fire,
flightless.

That loud hub of us,
meat stub of us, beating us
senseless.

Spectacular in its way,
its way of not seeing,
congealing dayless

but in everydayness.
In that hopeful haunting
(a lesser

way of saying
in darkness) there is
silencelessness

for the pressing question.
Heart, what art you?
War, star, part? Or less:

playing a part, staying apart
from the one who loves,
loveless.

Head Handed

Stop belonging to me so much, face-head.
Leave me to my child and my flowers.

I can't run with you hanging on to me like that.
It's like having ten dogs on a single lead

and no talent for creatures.
No hands, no trees. Not my dogs, nobody's.

Don't you have a place to go, face-head?
Deep into the brick basement of another life?

To kill some time, I mean. That furnace
light could take a shine to you.

There are always places, none of them mine.
And always time—rainbow sugar show

of jimmies falling from ice cream's sky—
but that stuff's extra, it's never in supply.

"Never," however, acres of it. Violet beans
and sarcasm. Too many flavors of it.

All those prodigal particles,
flimsily whimsical miracles, an embarrassment

of glitches. The chorus just *more us*.
But nowhere bare and slippery have I

got a prayer. If I had two hands
to rub together I wouldn't waste the air.

ALL POSSIBLE PAIN

Feelings seem like made-up things,
though I know they're not.

I don't understand why they lead me
around, why I can't explain to the cop

how the pot got in my car,
how my relationship

with god resembled that
of a prisoner and firing squad

and how I felt after I was shot.
Because then, the way I felt

was feelingless. I had no further
problems with authority.

I was free from the sharp
tongue of the boot of life,

from its scuffed leather toe.
My heart broken like a green bottle

in a parking lot. My life a parking lot,
ninety-eight degrees in the shade

but there is no shade,
never even a sliver.

What if all possible
pain was only the grief of truth?

The throb lingering
only in the exit wounds,

though the entries were the ones
that couldn't close. As if either of those

was the most real of an assortment
of realities—existing, documented,

hanging like the sentenced
under one sky's roof.

But my feelings, well,
they had no such proof.

Nemesis

The sun has its nemesis, evil twin star,
not its opposite but its spirit,
undead angel,

extra life. Another version.
The Andromeda Galaxy bears children
who become us, year after ancient,

ridiculous year. The children,
the alternatively filled selves unrecognizable
to our faeries, our animals and gods:

us utterly replaced.
The kids we were, rejected like organs
donated to the wrong body.

Why aren't they dear to us?
Why is that child least loved
by its own grown self?

If you aren't me then be banished from me,
weird orphan with limp and lisp.
Who, nameless brainsake, are you?

Not my substance or my shadow
but projectile vomit, a noxious gas.
Don't be me, please don't be me,

says the adult, looking back into wormhole
as if jumping into foxhole.
Not me, never again: that terrible child

with the insufferable littlesoul
and bad mom and sameself sister,
and balky, stalky brother

and monotone uncle and messed-with cousins,
and let's not even talk about the father,
the fater, pater, hated, fattened, late, latter dad.

Perhaps the Andromedans are such early
versions of us we can't hate yet, ghosts
or our pre-living selves, earliest babies.

Perhaps they're only life*like*, like
a robot cook or a motion detector,
not like a dog we love and know,

or claim to know,
who nonetheless attacks grandma
somehow. We say so, said so, toldya so.

That's what you get for believing in aliens,
for replacing our earhorn of plenty
with a megaphone of corpsedust.

Listen, it's moving closer, the Andromeda
Galaxy, this other us, this museum of mucus
and keyboards and keyboard fingertip records

that their governments are already optimized
to keep post-digitally. All of which looks
much more like a craps game to us, a hinky

life-filler, time-killer, the best selection of credit
card pill extensions with rapid-release hypo-air
no one but addicts can tolerate.

Only 2.5 million light-years away, lessening
daily, and that's collapsible
space, of course, made of light. Just flip

the switch and poof. We're there.
The space, then, the dog-run-sized length
between the golden retriever

and the Labrador retriever,
isn't so much space as time, and since time
is breath...well. Take a deep one.

We have all day, as a matter of objective fact.
Slip on a glossy patch of antimatter
and I've inhaled my unutterable

opposite potential self, smeared out
the tracing of my nemesis: Olympic
gymnast teen me or seventh-grade best friend

Shannon, or the cricket-eating
self-sister with the spiny-belled name I dream
at night and call out but can't ever know

in this world. Such a thing is called a soul?
A personality? Sometimes diagnosed "possession"?
Nemesis, namesake, nevermore.

O funny other self,
how I long to know you! You were ingested
so easily, absorbed like a lotion

in the desert. Even in the evening.
For there are no light years. Years are heavy.
There is only light. It never bends:

that's the property it mortgaged in order
to pick up speed. But parallel lines can meet
just like that if someone breaks the rules.

Some criminal sharing my name
or an alien name sharing my crime.
The rules are there are no rules. Lingua franca.

Isn't the space between what is
and what coulda woulda Buddha been,
that same space between short skull

and long face, that oiled jaw hinged
for supple expression, for saying
and blaming and braying and allaying

and naming: *I this* not *I that,* tit not tat,
want not waste, and *yes* not *yes, but...*
What your mother

tells you over and over to shut,
to smile, first to not talk to strangers
and then be kind to them.

To sponsor the tail of another winner's
horse. To Go for It.
To become something in this life.

But once the gardenias
are floating in seawater for the themed gala
of your body, this special night,

they are dying, bacteria or no bacteria,
life against life, this world
butted up against the next.

Simultaneity aside, we are all next.
All go to the light.
Heavily, with our childhoods we go.

I'll go with my stars,
and my sorry body, stranger
to myself, will say go.

THE WORLD'S ARM

A strong, pale wind on the thighs,
it was no seaspray, no AC,

but cold mnemonic, a breath
of spotless decision,

a kind of bulk, a true surface
thickened by foreign pears

as if winter brought its fruit
first to me for approval

before it let December
fill its basket to capacity.

I spoke too calmly for one
who didn't believe in anything.

Mouth full of pears,
full of promises I'd no way

to speak, much less keep, I tended
to gesture toward a Universal

Field of Grass, hoping to break
as many blades as my wide self

could in one pass. One pass—
but we're wasted with feeling,

breathing funny and stuck rough
like an IV into a paralyzed arm.

And that's the World's Arm
that can't write anymore,

or sign its name, or pick
the thickness from the trees.

My fingerprints transform
into proboscis, by degrees.

This Person-Sized Sky with Bruise,

simultaneously orange and violet
(though my eyes are closed), is

either my inner color (that covered mirror)
or simply dusk.

An opaline sheet
pulled because the night is ashamed

to come in front of everyone,
blacking out in joy.

Too shy to spill its milk on the stained
tablecloth of strangers

as I have. When it's finally dark
outside, it's finally

loose inside and the doubleness
of things seems too true to be good:

my way *and* the highway.
Night. It has two hands

I can use. Its fingers in a plum
too ripe not to split.

I had to split it. It was so much
itself—bloody flesh,

wild purple skin. A fistful
so lush it was almost imaginary,

smelling of love, it didn't matter whose.

Glassbottomed

Amplified blueness,
that is to say, I can hear it,
though it isn't music

or a voice but a self
apart from self itself. A handiwork.
Its horrible it-ness.

If only the plain brown splotch—
my home, my head—had a place,
a say, the way rancid meat still

has protein. Something to offer.
A little brown dog waves its paw
as if to say, I know all about it.

The it-ness. Broken into bits
so sharp everything gets cut to
sharp bits. Anything small has a kind

of integrity—whole, ridiculous—
god simply cannot have.
I mean, where's the magic

or the logic in being It
and hiding It? In seeing
foolishness, remaining wise?

Everyone's mouth of music
swallowed with salt. Oh, to be
in those waters when it matters.

A prayer is like a fishmouth,
opening dumbly onto just more
water at best or a hook

if it really wants an answer.
God (his blue holiness, his dry
drunk) is no real mystery,

unlike the wind-taut sail
and shining gulls and tiny souls
at everlasting work on the plain

brown boat in a bottle on the sea.

Streetlamps

The unplowed road is unusable
unless there's no snow.

But in dry, warm weather,
it's never called an unplowed road.

To call it so, when it isn't so,
doesn't make it so, though it is so

when it snows and there's no plow.
It's a no-go. Let's stay inside.

And here we are again:
no cake without breaking

eggs, unless it's a vegan cake
in which there are never any eggs

only the issue, the question,
the primacy of eggs,

which remains even in animal-free
foods, eaten by animal-free

humans in an inhumane world, lit
with robots breathing

powerlessly in nature.
O streetlamp,

wallflower clairvoyant,
you are so futuristically

old-fashioned,
existing in the daytime

for later, because it becomes
later eventually, then

earlier, then later again.
And a place is made

for that hope, if I call
it hope when half the time

is erased by the other half.
Light becomes itself

in the dark, and becomes
nothing when the real light

comes. It is enough to make
even the simplest organism

insane. Why did the chicken
cross the unplowed road?

Because it was trying
to beat the egg to the other side.

It wanted to be first,
at last, and to stay first,

at least until the day
breaks itself sunny side,

and the rooster crows.
The only snows are dark snows.

LIQUID FLESH

In a light chocolatine room
with blackout windows,
a loud clock drowns in soft dawn's

syllables, crisscrossed
with a broken cloudiness
I'd choose as my own bedcovers

but cannot. My choice of sleep
or sky has no music of its own.
There's no "its own" while the baby cries.

Oh, the baby cries. He howls and claws
like a wrongly minor red wolf
who doesn't know his mother.

I know I am his mother, but I can't
quite click on the word's essential aspects,
can't denude the flora

or disrobe the kind of housecoat
"mother" always is. Something
cunty, something used.

Whatever meaning the word itself
is covering, like underwear,
that meaning is so mere and meager

this morning. Mother. Baby.
Chicken and egg. It's so obnoxious
of me: I was an egg

who had an egg
and now I'm chicken,
as usual scooping up

both possibilities,
or what I used to call
possibilities. I used

to be this way, so ontologically
greedy, wanting to be it all.
Serves me right.

My belief in the fluidity
of the self turns out to mean
my me is a flow of wellwater,

without the well, or the bucket,
a hole dug and seeping.
A kind of unwell, where

the ground reabsorbs
what it was displaced to give.
The drain gives meaning to the sieve.

As I said: a chicken who still
wants to be all potential.
Someone who springs

and falls, who cannot see
how many of us I have
in me—and I do not like them all.

Do I like us? Can I love us?
If anyone comes
first it's him, but how can that be?

I was here way, way first.
I have the breasts, godawful, and he
the lungs and we share the despair.

For we are a we, aren't we? We split
a self in such a way that there isn't
enough for either of us.

The father of the baby is sleepy
and present in his way, in the way
of fathers. He is devoted like

few fathers and maybe hurts
like I hurt, like no fathers.
I don't know what someone else

feels, not even these someones
who are also me. Do they hurt
like I do? Why can't they

tell me, or morse or sign: let
me know they know where and how
and why it hurts? Or something?

What is the point of other people,
being so separate, if we can't
help a person get that pain

will stick its shiv into anything,
just to get rid of the weapon
and because it can? For if we share

ourselves then they, too, must
also be in so much pain.
I can hear it. Oh, my loves.

The wood of the crib, the white
glow of the milk (which must
have siphoned off the one

and only pure part of me, leaving
me with what, toxicity
or sin or mush?), the awful softness.

I've been melted into something
too easy to spill. I make more
and more of myself in order

to make more and more of the baby.
He takes it, this making. And somehow
he's made more of me, too.

I'm a mother now.
I run to the bathroom, run
to the kitchen, run to the crib

and I'm not even running.
These places just scare up as needed,
the wires that move my hands

to the sink, to the baby,
to the breast are electrical.
I'm in shock.

One must be in shock to say so,
as if one's own state is assessable,
like a car accident or Minnesota taxes.

A total disaster, this sack of liquid
flesh which yowls and leaks
and I'm talking about me

not the baby. Me, this puddle
of a middle, this utilized vessel,
cracked hull, divine

design. It's how it works. It's how
we all got here. Deform
following the function…

But what about me? I whisper
secretly and to think,
around these parts used to be

the joyful place of sex,
what is now this intimate
terror and squalor.

My eyes burned out at three a.m. and again
at six and eleven. This is why the clock
is drowning, as I said earlier.

I'm trying to explain it.
I repeat myself, or haven't I already?
Tiny self, alone with a tiny self.

I'll say it: he hurt me, this new
babe, then and now.
Perhaps he always will,

though thoughts of the future
seem like science fiction novels
I never finished reading.

Their ends like red nerves
chopped off by cleaver, not aliens,
this very moment, saving nothing for later.

He howls with such fury and clarity
I must believe him.
No god has the power

to make me believe anything,
yet I happen to know
this baby knows a way out.

This dark hole closing in on me
all around: he'll show me
how to get through

the shock and the godlessness
and the rictus of crushed flesh,
into the rest of my life.

2. DOUBLE LIFE

Parallel

The dark cracks separating
the white boards
think they're alone.

Why must I be burdened
with knowing
there are so many?

Or is this what god thinks?
Or am I what god thinks?
Or am I alone?

Visitor

I am dreaming of a house just like this one

but larger and opener to the trees, nighter

than day and higher than noon, and you,

visiting, knocking to get in, hoping for icy

milk or hot tea or whatever it is you like.

For each night is a long drink in a short glass.

A drink of blacksound water, such a rush

and fall of lonesome no form can contain it.

And if it isn't night yet, though I seem to

recall that it is, then it is not for everyone.

Did you receive my invitation? It is not

for everyone. Please come to my house

lit by leaf light. It's like a book with bright

pages filled with flocks and glens and groves

and overlooked by Pan, that seductive satyr

in whom the fish is also cooked. A book that

took too long to read but minutes to unread—

that is—to forget. Strange are the pages

thus. Nothing but the hope of company.

I made too much pie in expectation. I was

hoping to sit with you in a treehouse in a

nightgown in a real way. Did you receive

my invitation? Written in haste, before

leaf blinked out, before the idea fully formed.

An idea like a stormcloud that does not spill

or arrive but moves silently in a direction.

Like a dark book in a long life with a vague

hope in a wood house with an open door.

Why Should Only Cheaters and Liars Get Double Lives?

(a poem inside a poem)

That is, why should they get two stabs at it while the virtuous
trudge along at half-speed, half-mast, halfhearted?

If an ordinary human can pull the fattest cashwad
out of the slimmest slit,

and the fullest pudding out of the skimmest milk,
then it might be possible

to insert a meager life in Andromeda
into, at the very least, our wide pit of sleep.

Duplicity after all takes many, not merely two, forms,
and just the very idea

of doubleness, twinniness, or even simple, simpering
regret, or nostalgia, implies

a kind of Andromeda,
a secret world, the hidden draft, the tumor-sibling,

the "there-are-no-accidents" plane we could learn to fly.
There's always that irreducible "something extra"

to life on Earth:

> The way some men won't "talk that way" in front of women,
> not wanting to astonish us with their secret man-ness,
> as if there is another world bisecting ours,
> living among us like an unspeakable mold.

The recent invention of the double-decker pill,
equally effective on sunny *and* rainy days.

On the wall, a plural mural: a diptych of Paula 'n' Wally's.
What fallopian and what fellatio! Like a Nan Goldin oldie,
but an impostor. Okay. Why not try to offer more
squalor no matter who the photographer?

When someone's called a "lifer" it means that person is trapped.
A "lifer" has no real life but what do we call the rest of us?

How terrifying it is to try trying!
Which frying pan will best
kill the loved one? Which will
make the best omelet?

The books on the bookshelves are touching themselves
like virgins. But I've had them.

It Never Happened

Let's just imagine that you are magical,

that no light would flicker and no battery

die and no lover or wife or other can claim

you while you are with me. Let's imagine

that you shiver and shudder and eat

my lamb and my rice pudding and drink

the wine and the whiskey and the cognac

and the elderflower never taking your

eyes off me. Let's imagine that I am also

magical and can cook lamb and rice

pudding and pour many drinks without

ever taking my hands off you. Let's imagine

you are unable to control yourself when

we are together, that we are all thumbs

and soft mouths and terrible fingers

and eyes of moon and eyes of sea and that

we smell beautiful to each other for no

reason. Let's imagine you drove to my

house and your headlights did not flicker

and your battery did not die and you

were able to control the car and so

are not on the side of the road, not dead

or hurt but not anymore on your way

to my house either, calling your lover

or wife or other to come pick you up

and bring you home instead of coming

here, where there is no lamb, after all,

and no more wine, either, after all

this waiting, imagining you're magical,

imagining what you'd say to her: "Um,

I was on the other side of town to pick

up some wine for dinner" or "I was

meeting old buddy Tom for a drink, he's

just in town the one evening. Might

be home late." But you were never

coming over, never even invited. As if

I'd ever be so clever. In fact I was just

imagining you're magical when you called,

roadside, nearby, a blown battery for

no reason, for a ride home to your lover

or wife or other. You were on your way

home to her where she was preparing lamb

and rice pudding and when I dropped you

off you invited me in and I said no, not

taking my hands off the wheel, though

I wanted to imagine that your eyes flickered

and shivered and you said you couldn't

control yourself, couldn't take your eyes

off me, that I smelled like beautiful wine,

like elderflower, like pussy willow,

that you called me lamb and kissed me,

knowing that this very last part is the story's

only true part, in which you touched

and kissed me with your wheel of fingers,

your terrible lying mouth.

The Seven Deadly Sins of (and Necessary Steps toward) Making Art

Pure art is, in a sense, pure innocence.
But artists are, in themselves, putrid with paradox.

The following seven sins/steps should help the wretched
to remember: the pitfalls are the progress!

1. DEADLINES

Aka Avalanche Everlasting,
Opportunity Oppression.
"You will miss me then I'm gone…"

All at once a million kinds of calendar.

2. MOTIVATION

Ask yourself: What is my longing?
Answer yourself: I long for the world, in the form
of a person, which is me,
in the form of a new world,
in the form of a new person,
which is the new me, in the form…
ad infinitum.

3. GOALS

Stop staring out that old woman's window like a cat.

4. DISTINGUISHING BETWEEN "SAYING" AND "DOING"

"Everyone dies"
is different from
"Everyone died."

5. SELF-ABSORPTION

This inner spinning, that petty city
the mind built,

robs the psalm of its robe of calm,
my naked voice thin and shrill in the wind.

6. DELUSIONS OF GRANDEUR

I'm such a fraud
I can't even convince you
of my fraudulence.

7. EVERYDAY MAGIC!

The new burn on my knuckle,
white, shiny, raised:

our dinner's afterlife, lingering ghost.

Karaoke Realness at the Love Hotel

At the microphone, suddenly—oh no—
is Sandra the Available,

in her endless yellow dress
and award-winning earrings,

about to sing Rose Dickey's unrecorded
cakewreck of a hybrid poemsong,

"Sheep Child o' Mine."
Now watch her win the night

before it's all over. She's no loser
with a fever but no lover.

Not like me. I live in a hotel
with no rooms, just a lobby and lifts

leading to experiences.
Time to ask another person,

someone who's been outside
the fishbowl long enough

to wonder if there will ever again
be enough water. Rat race,

hamster wheel, dog run.
(Okay, dog run's different.

It's not for people.)
I'm not a real people-person.

Just like reality is not really realness,
people. Just try and point out to me

what's not fake or paste or false?
Or trick or replica

or denial or dream or drama
or simulation or reenactment

or knockoff or artificial, a ruse,
a work of art, illusion,

a lie, a mistake, fantasy,
a misconception, missed-connection,

delusion, hallucination,
insincere, invalid or invented,

a rehearsal with no performance?
A viable world with no excuse to exist?

In my hotel the sleep is free.
In any hotel. Why shouldn't it be?

And that old girl Sandra?
Turns out she can really sing.

Outfoxed

Red foxes are not allowed
to mate with white foxes
because the offspring
would all be female.

And we can't have that.
Blue foxes are not allowed
to mate with red foxes
because the offspring

would all be gay.
And we can't have that.
Brown foxes are not allowed
to mate with any other foxes

because the offspring would all
be, well, brown, in such variety
and number we'd never know
what was what anymore.

And we can't have that.

What we can have is affordable
fox fur, plentiful fox soup,
invigorating foxhunts
all brought to you by Fox News.

Inappropriate Dreams

I can't tell you
how often.

You in the grocery store
embarrassing

everyone with
the lettuce.

Elsewhere, food
in the file folders.

It's not supposed to
be there, get it?

Another time you
were rolling down a hill

like a blueberry
rolling toward

me, a bear who will
eat anything

this time of year
but wants

just you. Then
you are not you but

the plum of a pebble
that I skipped

into the lake
and found somehow

night after night.

PRODUCTS OF PERCEPTION

Perhaps an implantation.
Perhaps there is no soul. And biotech
metaphysics can't prove I'm whole.

If there were clear demarcation
between *me* and *why me*
then why wine and why whine

and if so, why not all the time?
Since flavor is olfactory
and pleasure in the brain,

does it make sense for the mouth
to open and admit blame?
Fluid body, fluent tongue,

flu-like symptoms hide a hole
through which a neutered fever catches
neutered cold. I'm told a kind of eerie light

flicks on when mind becomes itself.
Like when a book is opened,
and read, or just falls off the shelf.

MIRACLES

I spent the whole day
crying and writing, until
they became the same,

as when the planet covers the sun
with all its might and still
I can see it, or when one dead

body gives its heart
to a name on a list. A match.
A light. Sailing a signal

flare behind me for another to find.
A scratch on the page
is a supernatural act, one twisting

fire out of water, blood out of stone.
We can read us. We are not alone.

Big Game

after Richard Brautigan's
"A CandleLion Poem"

What began as wildfire ends up
on a candlewick. In reverse,
it is contained,

a lion head in a hunter's den.
Big Game.

Bigger than one I played
with matches and twigs and glass
in the shade.

When I was young, there was no sun
and I was afraid.

Now, in grownhood, I call the ghost
to my fragile table, my fleshy supper,
my tiny flame.

Not just any old but *the* ghost,
the last one I will be,

the future me,
finally the sharpest knife
in the drawer.

The pride is proud.
The crowd is loud, like garbage dumping

or how a brown bag ripping
sounds like a shout
that tells the town the house

is burning down.
Drowns out some small folded breath

of otherlife: O that of a lioness licking
her cubs to sleep
in a dream of savage gold.

O that roaring, not yet and yet
and not yet dead.

So many fires start in my head.

3. ARCANA

*Of one order are the mysteries of light
and of another are those of fantasy*

Rider Tarot Deck instructions

CARD 5: HIEROPHANT

I sit looking
around expectantly,
though really I want

nothing but I'm
so accustomed
to waiting around

I'll just take whatever
shows up. Or I look at
things I don't understand

and want them
though what I want
is understanding.

I take them anyway,
turning them over
and over in my hands

in the dark
as if holding such
things can give me

back some sense
of what it was like
to really want something

regardless of what
I had already
or how long I'd waited.

The wheels on the bus
go round and round.
Round and round.

But I am going nowhere.
I've not been waiting
for no bus.

Card 12: The Hanged Man

It seems unlikely that so much literature
could be made from twenty-six letters.
Doesn't it seem it could all be boiled
down to one sentence?

After all, the entire volatile cosmos
seems to circle and spin and rotate
so you'd think round and ellipse
were the only shapes possible.

You'd think a square was an ungodly
fluke, an aberration, not the life force
behind writing tables and scaffolding.
Not the product of a natural human math.

The kind of math that says: if you
are sentenced to be hanged
and the rope breaks in the middle
of your hanging, you are free to go.

Such a sentence, though uttered
without error, doesn't say what it
means: life may be a circle, but death's
elliptical, swinging and missing.

Criminal, hangman, judge, and witness,
each matchless and speechless. Why say
anything, ever again, after such luck?
Why not shut up and run?

Card 0: The Fool

Yes, you, fool. You don't fool
me, you fraud. *I'm* the fool.

I don't care. I run without
pants in winter, cock

tucked into my asshole
for warmth and a fun feeling.

It looks good, right? I take
my feet in my hands

and fringe the public scaffold
with my skunked stuff. Sexual

and digestive. It's so funny.
Are you embarrassed?

Why? You didn't do
anything but like it.

Foolish reader, can't like
what you like.

Like what you want to like.
Do what you want to like

to do. Don't do what you don't
want to like to do.

Card 20: Judgment

What did the stand of pines say
to the herd of elephants
wearing swimsuits
and carrying large suitcases?

"Nice trunks!"

Card 14: Temperance

The everyday truth
of the night's delectations
appears for us in our dream.

We all ate the same food
and made the same love
so we dream the same dream,

which was: the infinite wine
was rank, undrinkable, lost
to a rot somehow familiar,

a delusion or virus, perhaps
from childhood, parents
deep in their cups.

It could have been worse.
Upon waking, we might not
have had or needed wine.

Card 7: The Chariot

I smoke between one and three
cigarettes a day.

Sometimes a whole pack will last
a week, sometimes three

or sometimes I don't keep track,
just give them all away.

I can always get them back.
There isn't a tree

on the street I haven't given
the time of day.

Time for us to meet, or maybe
eat, between one and three.

A cigarette or two or three
with you can't be beat.

And sometimes I forget to eat,
forget the pack, and that too

is okay, you always say.
What other way, but to

forget, is there to endure
the day, the street?

Card 9: The Hermit

I burned a living rose in the fire,
its fleshsmell human.

The baby's breath also reeked
burnt. I learned the tarot

in one sitting—arcana slipping
into my mind like a beloved

hand under my pillow.
When I woke I was so hungry

I ate the last pear. Last for the year,
another rotten year in which

I don't need to save the pear for you.
It didn't matter how I sat with you.

I didn't have to cover my thighs
or make attractive angles.

I could look like a black spider
with flesh pockets

or a hairy, scrambled woman
and you would reach for even that.

I burned the pillow too,
so many objects here in the cabin

seemed to me akimbo
and interlocking. I put

everything in the fire
because it was too confusing.

Card 16: The Tower

What did the fatal illness say
to the nonfatal illness?

"Are you still working on that platelet
or can I get rid of it for you?"

Card 19: The Sun

When you show yourself to the woman
you love, you don't know your fear

is not fear itself. You have never been good,
but now you are so good,

who are you? Is it the liquidity of her skin
that bathes the world for you,

or her face, captured like a she-lion
in your own flesh?

This summerbed is soft with ring upon ring
upon ring of wedding, the kind

that doesn't clink upon contact, the kind
with no contract,

the kind in which the gold is only (only!) light.
Cloud covers and lifts,

and sleep and night, and soon enough
love's big fire laughs at a terrible burn,

but only (only!) because pain absorbs excess
joy and you shouldn't flaunt

your treasures in front of all day's eyes.

CARD 6: THE LOVERS

When standing naked, no mirror,
this is just me. Just me, justly
before a lover who breaks

this wholeness as if
he were a mirror
but with his mouth.

When you say I am beautiful
suddenly I stop being so
because you have claimed that.

Card 17: The Star

I know where you go when you're hoping
to be happy: to your large, dark envelope,

pricking points of light with your tiny pin.
You call us stars, and use infantile words

like twinkle and wish, and faraway. But we're far
from far. We're in. And we're old.

We're the deep, hot gleam in your wet, cold holes.
We call them "eyes." They are our only homes.

We shine nowhere else. The sky is a smother
of blank dust and explosion and vapor.

In your "eyes" we see fear, what you call sparkle.
We know it's fear because we already died. We know

how it felt. Listen: I am dead and you can't see it.
Do you know what this says about us both?

I'm begging: please choose me to be your star.
Wish on me. Love the oh-yes of my being dead

enough to call it brightness. If I can't be yours,
I am just a dark scar pulling the skin of the sky,

unnerved and fallen from the reach of your amazed
groping dream that everything lives twice.

That dream hurts me the best. I depend on it.
Get a new envelope and make one new pinhole.

Just one hole. Don't try to save the others.
Don't bother. I'm the lucky one. It's me. Me!

Card 8: Strength

What did god say
to the friendless woman whose child
was ill and whose home was lost?

"And it's only Wednesday!"

4. FAMILY TRIP

Family Trip

We never knew closer
sisters, stronger trees,
tighter clans, wilder
fires. Where can we
go if not to each other,
resenting every step?

I Wish I Had More Sisters

I wish I had more sisters,
enough to fight with and still
have plenty more to confess to,
embellishing the fight so that I
look like I'm right and then turn
all my sisters, one by one, against
my sister. One sister will be so bad
the rest of us will have a purpose
in bringing her back to where
it's good (with us) and we'll feel
useful, and she will feel loved.

Then another sister
will have a tragedy, and again,
we will unite in our grief, judging
her much less than we did the bad
sister. This time it was not
our sister's fault. This time
it could have happened to any
of us and in a way it did. We'll
know she wasn't the only
sister to suffer. We all suffer
with our choices, and we
all have our choice of sisters.

My sisters will seem like a bunch
of alternate me, all the ways
I could have gone. I could see
how things pan out without
having to do the things myself.
The abortions, the divorces,
the arson, swindles, poison jelly.
But who could say they weren't

myself, we are so close. I mean,
who can tell the difference?

I could choose to be a fisherman's
wife since I'd be able to visit
my sister in her mansion, sipping
bubbly for once, braying
to the others who weren't invited.
I could be a traveler, a seer,
a poet, a potter, a flyswatter.
None of those choices would be
as desperate as they seem now.
My life would be like one finger
on a hand, a beautiful, usable, ringed,
wrung, piano-and-dishpan hand.

There would be both more and less
of me to have to bear. None of us
would be forced to be stronger
than we could be. Each of us could
be all of us. The pretty one.
The smart one. The bitter one.
The unaccountably-happy-
for-no-reason one. I could be,
for example, the hopeless
one, and the next day my sister
would take my place, and I would
hold her up until my arms gave way
and another sister would relieve me.

MAGI

If only you'd been a better mother.

How could I have been a better mother?
I would have needed a better self,
and that is a gift I never received.

So you're saying it's someone else's fault?

The gift of having had a better mother myself,
my own mother having had a better mother herself.
The gift that keeps on not being given.

Who was supposed to give it?

How am I supposed to know?

Well, how am I supposed to live?

I suppose you must live as if you had been
given better to live with. Comb your hair, for instance.

I cut off my hair, to sell for the money
to buy you what you wanted.

I wanted nothing but your happiness.

I can't give you that!
What would Jesus do?
He had a weird mother too...

Use the myrrh, the frankincense, as if
it were given unconditionally, your birthright.

It's a riddle.

All gifts are a riddle, all lives are
in the middle of mother-lives.

But it's always winter in this world.
There is no end to ending.

The season of giving, the season
when the bears are never cold,
because they are sleeping.

The bears are never cold, Mama,
but I am one cold, cold bear.

My Water Children

They could have been anyone,
no one special. I didn't need

them to be angels or stars.
But to me, they were a boy

and twin girls. Like ink soaking
through from the other side

of the page I write on now,
they form no images, no story.

A crack in the wall admitted
no spider, no draft, but only

because there was no wall.
Often, as a child, when I did

something wrong and got away
with it, I thought a ghost

or spirit or a kind of assistant
god (not the Real God, who was

too busy for the souls of children
and it turns out that is true)

would bleed through to me
from the skin of the other world,

cut by my misdeed or sin,
and catch me. I wanted to be seen,

known for what I truly was:
a bad child, unlike the perfect

water children I would never have
the chance to know.

VACATION

for Mark and Paul

1

When the mind walks without language,
there is no boardwalk; there is no Board;
there is no boredom; and there are no feet,
legs or yards, coin or meter. No measure,
no miles. What is freedom if not freedom
from distance? From speaking lines?

2

The leaves, little green lamps for the sunblind.

3

Blue fingertips. Could mean a beach-party
manicure or a corpse. Or: *and* a corpse.
To be touched intimately by blue fingertips.
To put it more bluntly: to be fingered
by the pool in which you drown.

4

Why not sparkle if given a choice and you've
had enough sleep? Why not give back
a tiny grain of what you've been given from
night's endlessness and guaranteed breathing?
I have fractured only so minute a corner
of the deadest, most useless bone in the sky's
body, how can I not make a kite of it?

How can I keep even the broken glass
to myself, drinking nothing out of nothing?

5

To swim is to let god know you won't take it
lying down nor will you just lie down and take it.

6

Solemn toes respond directly even to the most
frivolous mind. What other rules but bent
rules? Can I love you from the other
side of the conversation? From the other side
of the brown-feathered space of the table?
Of the living, eaten egg and sunrise and sleep-
eyes wet from night?

7

The tiny grain of sand in the eye. The single
flap that lands the bird into the lonely next,
the only nest in the sea. The glimmer that
proves contact has been made. Dear child,
wild sea, closed eye. Far, loving air.

8

Walking in the sand—am I under the sun
or dangling over it, first by one foot
and then the other?

9

This cerulean weather and its yellow talons.
The afternoon on the brink of drink. My ears
are plugged with wax and seawater, utterly
corked. The light has to widen to include
the music I can't hear. I am hoping the god
of catastrophe—barbecue, lightning, riptide—
has smarter fish to fry. Suddenly the scruffy
deer appears, as it often does in poems, a dark-
eyed child dreaming in a dream.

10

Where oh where is that *one leaf?*

COVER THE LAMP WITH ITS OWN LIGHT

Though I am well,
and deep, and fall asleep well,

I am not the wisher that I am.
I think that just thinking about

lighting the way and lighting
a match are the same thing,

is the same thing as doing either.
With both hands the same thing

and that thing is me. But it's
all the time, every day. But no.

It's not for me to say.
It's not heatlight's way to have

me in heatlight's way saying
no light today or heat will pay.

When golden oak leaves, real
gold, real leaf, flaked thickly

all over my wonderful dull self
with a gleam like fresh paper

what did the old boulder say,
in a waste of words?

"Some kind of freak lives next door,
a fish-striped alien

on an earplug binge who simply
will not acknowledge she's being

called home." Home! Home!
But nobody's called me, nobody's

home. There isn't even a phone.
Perhaps I'll start working alone,

on two separate films,
enrobed in a copycat

body, a leaping projection,
for isn't that what we do?

Leap. A larger footprint
than creature. An aluminum

filling doubling as a bulletproof
vest that's been tested

as a way out through the window.
The window of curved mirror,

of salt, the window of it all,
the latched feeling,

to quit patching the baby,
for example (did you know

there was a baby? You'd think
he'd be mentioned by now,

but the things I choose not to say
might keep you wondering to the end

of the page, the fat page, the fat
unmentionable this and that),

onto the habit of the baby.
Where is the quilt? The boulder-

edged quilt. The one used for Earth
Day. The stained, strange,

fleshlike quilt, fortress, green-feared,
many-colored dress.

It was my costume,
it was my stained-red pink thing

all last year. It was my rag doll
concubine shrink honey

girlfriend hag that I had to have
at home or I wouldn't go home.

If my wish is anything more
than a graft, a draft,

a cover, ten thousand lovers
in the space of one, then I will take

all three: these wishes: baby,
body, poem. Or body, hobby,

bone. And make them as true
as a genie can make them come.

True as a field in lamplight,
as a stone believing it's all alone.

With my wishes I can kill them
twice, and still get them back:

maybe, body, prone.
Unbelievable that it is still today.

How much more of it is left?
How much more of tomorrow?

I am not greedy. I ask because
I hope for less than I have coming.

I am not more than I hoped
to be in my prayers

in my girlhood, in my bonfire.
Not in my ungodly unuttered

then-ness. If that old boulder
ever lived a day with any burden

but itself then I will lift its hard-
meat to a place of honor.

Super-polished on the very top
of the world's biggest root.

I am not ungrateful. I will face
the stranger's face in any light

from any lamp or lucky gold
three-wish thing. I will not

wish for two things and then use
the third wish for three more.

I won't take more than I have,
and I don't have to want

what I already have from before.
It's too quiet and sorry to want,

and the place of wanting is too sore
to stuff it with hard rock,

hard luck, or it's too far back
to even see the stuff anymore.

I'm open. I'm old. I just want
the wishing to go back home

or to send me back, in its place,
to where the giving is given out.

Mermaid's Purse

There is no such thing as sacrifice,
though the bleeding doesn't end.

The self is the self yet bigger than itself.
Indebted. And subordinate

to the unity of its fragments,
loopholes in the loop of wholeness.

Cat sharks lay their eggsacs,
which eat themselves in gestation,

for if fewer mature sharks,
bigger portions at the feast

of the loggerhead turtle, which
will never again be a single entity.

Out of one, many. If blameless,
then meaningless, dissolved

by a cloud of sardines, flashing
silver as if paying for breakfast

in a silent movie starring no stars.

VANITY

To think that, in my sorrow,
I thought it was permissible to flick
myself away like a fly from the full-length

mirror on opening night. Curled the hot
hair around my crowded face,
warming up the audience for a flop.

I thought I'd be bought something,
by one who admired me. Some lost meal,
hours of fat drink check, a copselike rope

of rubies for my waist. But no. I'm selfsame:
a wordsmith wearing too much paint,
my inking irons heavy in the rain.

The night is an imperfect story
for us all. It leaves things out.
The witch's song can't prove itself

beautiful enough to sing at dawn
for the enchanted child
in an ordinary story about the night.

No small favor, no laughing matter.
Pass the meat through a slot
in the chamber. This whole self

can be as silent as a chain saw rusted
on the broken fever of my song's rain,
my night's story, my ink iron's brains.

In spite of the spot-checking,
the self-seeking, the meticulous soul-smithing,
I am still me, lacking.

Like murders in books, but with reverse
precision, how anyone becomes herself
is a mystery. A miracle. A myth.

5. OUR ANDROMEDA

At the Book Shrink

one learns to say "My body uses me
as a grape uses wine"—

to talk about inevitability,
the essence of plot.

But what happens when a person
understands she is being sent

back, glass by glass,
to the invisible pouring stations

of the larger narrative?
That she is merely like or likely

a person in a book?
Like a saltwater balloon

sinking in the ocean.
Like a person in a book, like

I said already. Someone's
not listening. Someone's

eating breakfast or falling
asleep or texting a married lover

as shrinks are wont to do.
If I am boring then at least

I am getting somewhere:
through the wood I knock on.

My story is telling.
But it's not telling *me*.

I need help getting to the next part.
When I open my mouth,

liquid rushes in, endrunkening.
When I close it,

dark, secret-looking drops spill
crimson on the page.

HEADLONG

Be strange to yourself,
in your love, your grief.

Your wet eyelashes a black
fringe on brown pain

and your feet unbelievably
sure, somehow, surfing

your own shadow,
that too-large one cresting

just now, too soon for you
to get inside the curl:

the one place in the ocean
where it's safe. And safe

only for a half-breath
(a fish's sip with
hooked lip),

only for that one blink
of an eye already shut (tiptoe

to the foreshadow) against
the headlong wall of salt water.

To My Twenty-Three-Year-Old Self

The woman you think
Is the love of your life

Is only a way to get
To New York City.

I probably shouldn't
Say that until she leaves

You. Because you will
Hate me if I say it now.

You "love" "her" so
Much. You are lavishing

A lifetime of unexpressed love
On this poor expressionless

Child. She can barely feel.
And you, you narcissist,

You can only feel yourself.
If you really loved her,

You would try to help her.
But in the end, I'm glad

You spent your energies
Writing love poems and

Trying to transform your love
Into art. It worked out

For you. FSG will buy it
Even though it's juvenile.

You'd believe that before
You'd believe she'll leave you.

In six weeks. Without a trace.
Saying: *You don't know who*

You are. And besides you're not
Butch enough for me.

As if you wouldn't make yourself
Into *anything* for her.

Had she only said she wanted it.
Luckily for you, she didn't.

To My Twenty-Four-Year-Old Self

You wouldn't know me,
If I came to you in a dream.

You'd be sleeping
It off, you'd be naked

And cute, but you think
You're a kind of monster

And maybe you are,
Just not an ugly one.

That whole business
Will come later.

You'd pass me on the street
As well, a "normal,"

Someone who traded
In her essentials for

A look of haunted
Responsibility.

Someone who was maybe
Once a girl you'd know.

I would want to tell
You that romance

Was a kind of civilization
That fell. I cannot

Explain the complex
Strategies in that bitter

Defeat, not that I
Fathom it, except to say

That we are all haunted.
You too, in your wild love

And fear. You are a monster.
I am not a dream.

To My Twenty-Five-Year-Old Self

Billy Collins, have you any
Idea how important

You were to my twenty-five-year-
Old self? You weren't

Poet laureate yet, you
Were just a teacher I had

In Ireland. You were
Expansive and you

Believed in me.
I felt like a real poet

With you for the first
Time even though we

Argued about feminism
And things that mattered.

I was just at that cusp
Of being someone who wanted

So desperately to write,
Tipping over into becoming a writer.

I was fighting it. I didn't know
How to be except angry.

I was frightened. What if I
Could be good? What if

I would never be good?
Would your attention

Be all I'd ever really have
Of poetry? How could I know?

And so I was angry at you.
And between the lesbian

Love I'd left in New York
Who, I'm grateful, convinced

Me to buy contact lenses
So I could see the green

Hills, and the British physicist
I'd end up in bed with

Before I'd left Ireland,
There was something pure

And aboveboard, not teacherly
But generous, and lovely

And incomplete and no
One thing. I won't forget it:

The way you laughed
At some mean joke, at some

Ugly truth, into the wind
So it blew back into our happy,

Stupid faces on a ferry made me understand,
This is love the way poets know it.

To My Thirty-Eight-Year-Old Self

Calvin will be fine,
I want to say

To this woman who
Is one year older than me.

To tell her: You may still
Not be able to tell,

But he will catch up,
And fit into the category

Of "normal" and we'll
Both laugh at ourselves,

Who never imagined
Normal as a good thing

For anybody, much less
A beautiful, innocent

Baby. Who has a real
Chance at being magnificent.

She'll say what
Did we know…we were

So worried. Still though,
If anyone ever makes

Fun of him, calls him
Stupid or a spaz

Or anything, I'm sure
Even our eighty-five-year-old

Self, we at our big
Wisdom-apex age,

Will vivisect that anyone
With a grapefruit spoon.

We'll laugh, but then
She'll turn to me and say:

But you're from the past.
You're just me last year.

You don't know
Any more than I do.

In fact, she'll say,
Backing away,

You know even less.
You're fucking with me.

Then she won't let me
Touch her or say another

Word. So what was
The point of my coming here?

THE NEW PEOPLE

I had no desire to get to know the screamers,
our loud-in-ten-ways, annoying, drunk and boorish
neighbors, but I didn't put up

a fence or anything. Didn't fight it
when they brought us plates of their fatty meals
and overlong chitchat. We were new,

just renting, and I didn't want to be rude,
either, when Joanna and Vince
brought us their statue of the Virgin Mary

when our newborn son was in the hospital.
Joanna had tears in her eyes and though I am not
Catholic, or even Christian—or not

anymore anyway, I think, if it's like what I suppose
in that you have to keep up with the dues
to stay in the club—

I accepted the statue. I took in the alien
mother and wrapped her in a blanket.
I lay her on a low shelf and broke

the news to my Jewish husband, who cringed
and said, "She gave you *what?*"
But I didn't care

what it was, from what god or goddess
or neighbor or creature or kiln.
I was becoming someone I didn't know

each day without my little boy—near insanity
about his tiny, pure, hurt self. All those wires.
Blessed Virgin Mary, Mother of God,

Holy Statue in my baby's silent room, I promise
I will believe in you, and in Jesus too. Please...
Why was I cradling a "mother" statue,

a ceramic doll, this creepy relic,
instead of my living, beautiful son?
If *she* could make it all the way here,

across so many territories of indifference,
into my most secret empty room—
surely my child, who belonged, would come home soon?

If You So Much As Lay a Hand

What can I possibly understand
holding on to the idea that he is mine?

Denying the fact that he's really being passed
from hand of the living to hand of the dead
above my head

in a game of keep-away
in which I am not the mother who makes
the rules and has her say

but the target, who makes them all laugh
at my attempts to stay light-

hearted, game, so the teasing
doesn't turn more vicious.

If some clumsy god drops him
or forgets to wind up his breath
enough to last the whole night

or if some irritated hand swats him away
like a fly, I will replace my life

with blood sport, wild to find that arm,
the tendoned shoulder, the loose fist of that god,

aim for his face, his expression. I will see it.
See whether he equals in horror
my child's beauty.

Whether there is light in his eyes,
or envy. If there are such hands,
such a brutal face

to my son's luck or unluck.
The words flog and flay and no mercy
come to mind, like some maniac order

divinity believes only it can give,
or dissolve like a membrane

between world and love.
A jellyfish can find, in water,
the air it needs

to keep the poison ready. Even if
this god is not some creature,
with creature-logic

and animal heft, but only an idea
the breath forms from death,

from a random plot of book or land,
not man or kind of man,

if I so much as see the shadow
of that hand.

NACHTRÄGLICHKEIT

after Kaja Silverman's
Flesh of My Flesh

On having slashed myself from throat to instep
in one unbroken line,

I suppose it was a reenactment, Freud's *Nachträglichkeit:*
the second act. The past presses so hard

on the present, the present is badly bruised,
blood brims under the skin.

That was the situation I was in. Wearing a jacket of blood
from an earlier crime,

which was also mine. A curving zipper with misaligned
teeth, open to show red lipstick,

meat. And a stage smile, have a seat! Normally I'm much
more careful, naturally something

like this would only ever happen in a dream,
but even dreams have their dreams

of finding their dreamer awake, silent within earshot,
carving knife in hand.

Did you know that anguish thins the blood and thickens
the vessel? It was like cutting

a rare steak. A minotaur, glittering with rubies
and pink candles. My hands hung

like electrical wires off a building on the edge of collapse,
every one of my gestures symbolic,

ruined of magic. For there is no miraculous beast,
and there never was, standing

on the golden field of frozen honey clover,
each leaf strong enough to bend

under everything's weight. Strong because it bends.
Because it has already been crushed,

but its cells know that blight, one massive cut,
will slit each tiny skin surgically

in order to save the field from itself. I cannot suffer
the same fate twice, force my own hand

or stay it. Can't repeat or unrepeat. This finitude
is infinite and infinitely expanding.

Hearth

Love comes from ferocious love
or a ferocious lack of love, child.

A *to* and a *from,* and an urgency,
a barefoot sprint in the high snow

for the only sagging shack in sight.
No doctor runs through the winter

woods at midnight to bring placebo.
But when he does it's just too late—

the house all fevered, grief the very
gifts of milk and stew and hearth

offered anyhow. How many tree
limbs are amputated by the self-

important sudden surgery of a gale—
those same limbs tortured further,

re-galed, as spirit-dancing fire?
But the trees don't experience it

the way it seems to me, like how
all that individual snow clumps

together because it is lonely
and trusts its kind. To be home

is to go somewhere, is velocity,
the same urgent comfort

of your name. You'll lack nothing,
child, and I will never let you go.

HIDE-AND-SEEK WITH GOD

There are no hiding places left, Cal.
Every dark space isn't really dark
but pinkish black, flesh and oblivion,
filled with me, with us, deathly
and breathless and holding on, skin
about to split and give us away.

Is it better to run? Run down
the street—the floating red hand
that means *don't walk* looks
like a heart. But I'm too afraid.
If we just close our eyes truly enough,
believing hard, no peeking, we can
be invisible. Don't let him find
us, Cal. Don't let him find us again.

OUR ANDROMEDA

When we get to Andromeda, Cal,
you'll have the babyhood you deserved,
all the groping at light sockets

and putting sand in your mouth
and learning to say *Mama* and *I want*
and sprinting down the yard

as if to show me how you were leaving
me for the newest outpost of Cal.
You'll get the chance to walk

without pain, as if such a thing
were a matter of choosing a song
over a book, of napping at noon

instead of fighting it. You'll have
the chance to fight every nap,
every grown-up decision that bugs

you, and it will be a fair fight, this time,
Cal, in Andromeda. You will win.

•

In Andromeda there would be no
sleepy midwife who doesn't know
her own weakness, no attending

nurse who defers like a serf
to the sleepy midwife, no absent
obstetrician, no fetal heart monitor

broken and ignored, no sloppy
hospital where everyone checks
their own boxes and only consults

the check marks when making
decisions that will hurt us, Cal.
None of those individual segments

will be there in Andromeda,
no segments to constitute the worm
that burrowed into our bodies

and almost killed us. The worm
that is supposed to return us back
to Earth is supposed to come after

we die, not when we are giving birth
and being born. But even in the Milky
Way, we did manage to get you born;

and I will never forget the spark,
the ping of mind, the sudden gift
from nowhere that told me what I had

to do to push you out. I had
no force left in me but a voice
in my head, "Love. Love!" A command.

The kind of love we cannot understand,
so concentrated that had it been made
of blood it would be compressed

into a pure black diamond
as large as a galaxy and as heavy
as a crushed star.

The eye would explode from looking at it.
The mouth would attach itself
like a leech and fall off, dead.

LOVE. Over and over that voice told me
what to think and do and what to use
and finally, it worked.

It cracked me open with the muscle
of a Roman god's shattering
fist and it was the god of war or the sea

called in for the emergency, on alien
wires by some Andromedan operator.
That is how you were born.

You were hardly alive, hardly you,
horribly slim-chanced. I blacked out
hard but I heard you were blue.

That voice that told me what to do
came from Andromeda. It's the only truth.
There wasn't a soul in that hospital

room told me a single thing anywhere
near as true. It was Andromedan
love that delivered you.

•

Wait till you see the doctors in Andromeda,
Cal. Yes, the doctors. It's not the afterlife,
after all, but a different life.

The doctors are whole-organism empaths,
a little like Troi on *The Next Generation*
but with gifts in all areas of the sensate self.

Not just mental or emotional empathy
but physiological. The doctors know how
you feel. They put their hands on you

and their own spleen aches, or their spirit
is tired, tendon bruised, breast malignanced,
et cetera. The patient's ills course

through the doctor's body as information,
reliable at last. There are no misdiagnoses
or cursory dismissals as if the patient

were a whiny dog who demands another
biscuit. Or shooting in the dark like good
Dr. Shtep in the NICU, when you were

trying to begin living, who asked me
whether I had taken street drugs. What else
could explain your catastrophic entrance

into the human fold of the Milky Way
but the gross ignorance and disregard
of me, not her colleagues? Not even a god

we'd never share. The doctors there
are more like angels are supposed to be,
when they breathe you can sleep peacefully.

You might be surprised to hear that illness
occurs on Andromeda. That the field
of medicine is still a necessary patch of land.

Did you think I was telling you a fairy tale,
Cal? Trying to get some religious parables
into your already impassioned childhood

and indoctrinate you toward the obligations
of heaven? I am not. People still get sick
in Andromeda, and woe and death

and grief arrive each day like packets
of mail through a slot in the door.
How could it be otherwise? It is life,

after all. And despite what the religious
on Earth try to prove, no one can choose
life. We can only choose choices.

●

People get sick in Andromeda.
The difference is that people taking
care of the sick don't pretend

they know what they do not
and cannot know. In Andromeda,
everybody knows what they

need to know. Even doctors,
even patients. Even, yes, insurance
companies that don't even use

the word "claim," certainly not in the form
of a form, in their business,
because it's just rude and heartless

to hurt further a hurt person by making
them shout in the wind, wondering
whether their pain will be approved, deemed

real, awarded validation in the form
of not bankrupting the sufferer instantly
with avalanching bills. They know that there.

We don't even need to pack our bags,
Cal. I can't be sure but how much
you want to bet they have better bags, too?

•

You'll learn to read so much more easily there,
Cal! You'll be able to see the letters
better in that atmosphere.

Maybe their alphabet has twenty-six, or maybe
thousands like Chinese characters.
It won't matter because your vision

will delineate even the finest fifteen-stroke
pictogram and you will laugh and laugh
at how the letter O looks like an open mouth

in your old language. How childish that will
seem! Your beautiful eyes may change color
with all the perfect seeing you do.

Maybe we'll miss the aqua ring around
sandy-colored irises flecked with gray and green,
little tropical islands studded

with prehistoric boulders and effusive flora,
encircled by rich, bright ocean.
Perhaps the new air in Andromeda will turn

them into brown and gray buildings,
a city in which to flick on all the lights
in a skyscraper so you can read

so far into the night I call from the next room:
"That's enough, Cal. The book will still
be there tomorrow. Time for sleep."

●

And yes, Cal, you can roll your eyes at me,
your frumpy old mom with her wacky
ideas. I do believe in Andromeda.

You don't have to. I'll believe hard enough
for the both of us.
Because it's all my fault, you see.

I'm the one who joined that cult
of expectant mothers
who felt ourselves too delicate

and optimistic to *entertain the notion,*
as if I were inviting it to an unpleasant
afternoon tea, of something going wrong

with the birth of my child. Like so many
others, I thought it wouldn't happen
to me. In a way, it didn't happen to me.

It happened to you. And because
I wouldn't invite the terrible guests
into my psyche for goddamned tea,

I wasn't careful enough. I thought
my experience of childbirth
was a consideration. I thought

I was playing it safe by having the Best
Midwife, one who truly understood
the beauty and horror of childbirth

and who would take my side
in the ordeal (I didn't know that meant
she'd take my side *against you!*)

and who would be like a sister
to me, an expert sister and nurse and doctor
and goddess of natal wisdom

all in one, with the extra precaution
of planning to deliver in a hospital,
in case the tea-guests arrived

without invitation. I thought the hospital
was a real hospital, too. That it knew
what it was doing and had a legal

and moral obligation to know
what it was doing. I thought that
since I was so healthy, and you were

growing so beautifully, and all the tests
and charts and balances were perfect,
that I was doing everything right.

I was arrogant. I was selfish. I wanted
to do it all correctly as if I were building
a model birdhouse at summer camp.

I was wrong. I was wrong to see the other
new mothers sighing over their sore
perinea and healthy infants

and believe that I would be like them.
Since when have I ever believed I was like
anyone else? Only when it served me,

Cal. I can blame just about anyone for what
happened to you, but ultimately it was my job
to get you into this world safely. And I failed.

There is no other way to look at it.
The other day I was walking down Court Street
in my neighborhood and saw a mother,

her child in a stroller. We were all stopped at
the same corner, waiting for the light
to change, to cross the street.

The mother was craning her neck to the left
to watch for cars, her stroller pushed out
so far ahead of her it was already

in the street, ready to go, when an unseen car
zipped fast past us, dangerously close
to her child, and the first thing the mother did

was turn to me and say, panicked,
"Did you see that? He didn't even have the light!"
But I couldn't feel any sympathy for her.

In fact, I recoiled from her safe and lucky outrage.
It's not the driver's fucking job to ensure
her child grows up safely. She could be right

and the driver wrong and her kid dead.
Two out of three is what happened instead.
She should hold him a little tighter

than usual and not waste this lesson
on being angry at a car. But I said nothing,
and, disgusted, wasted my own anger on her.

·

I suppose I could blame God. That's what cowards
do, the lazy. Like people who pretend to be
so abysmally unskilled at cooking

that someone else feeds them throughout life.
Those people are always the pickiest eaters,
have you noticed?

But let's say I won't eat potato or dairy and I can't
tolerate onion, eggs or wheat,
what exactly would I be blaming God for?

A mistake, misjudgment, an oversight (a word
that has always amused me, its simultaneously
opposite meanings) or utter cruelty?

Weakness? Naptime? Drunk driving?
Vengefulness? Power-madness? Experimenting
with karma, playing with matches,

autopilot? Stupidity, quotas, just taking
orders? Mixing up the card files Comedy
and Tragedy? An inept assistant who

has since been fired? Poor people-skills?
Forgetfulness? Had a headache?
A cover-up? Setting things in motion so that

this poem would be written? Overworked,
underpaid? The system being broken?
Technical difficulties? Couldn't find remote?

Track-work, electrical storm, hurricane,
prayer-lines jammed by the devout,
new policies, change of direction within

the administration? On vacation, paternity
leave, sick leave, personal day, long-term
disability, short-term disability, layoffs?

Who am I to underestimate God in this way?
To imply he's some bumbling Joe,
working stiff trying to do an honest day's work?

I mean really. Who knows his workings?
If I don't know what to blame him for,
how can I blame him at all?

Perhaps there was never a flaw in the first place,
no mistakes. Perhaps God is perfect,
utterly blameless. He is what he is. Evil.

•

The gods of Andromeda, however benevolent,
cannot answer unless called.

They don't operate like Milky Way God,
who doesn't answer at all,

who is always busy offline, jetskiing
on our waterbodies, our handsqueezed

oceans of salt water, competing in dressage
though he always spooks the horses.

In those days when I would call and call
into the stupid air, if I ate something

sweet I would begin to cry, overwhelmed
by how small comfort had become.

●

So you see, Cal, we're not in particularly
good hands here. Not mine, helpless
and late, not even yours,

tiny, graceful stations the train lines
keep skipping though we've all
been waiting in the rain.

We will find our kind in Andromeda,
we will become our true selves.
I will be the mother who

never hurt you, and you will have your
childhood back in full blossom,
whole hog. We might not know

who we are at first, there, without
our terrible pain. But no flower
knows the ocean.

The sea can never find the forest,
though it can see the trees.
The succulent has no bud for salt

but one mile away the deer lick
and lick as if the sea
were in its newborn body,

replenishing the kelp of the hoof.
Though a sea would as soon
drown a deer as regenerate it,

there's a patch of mercy, sweetly
skewing between the two.
The new wind is already in us, older sister

to us all, blowing windfall and garbage
alike to those who do not deserve
either gifts or refuse.

●

And then of course, there were the friends.
It's amazing how the ones without children
leapt to their feet in anguish

and keened, utterly genuine and broken,
made their way to our apartment with stews
and wine and tears, fruit and olive oil

and kindness so beautiful it wasn't of this world.
While our own families, our parents,
seemed so stunned (as if by a stun gun)

by their own fear that they receded
into an ether, the veiled planet Venus
for all I understood, some bright

occasional visitation and months
of silence. And, oh, the friends with precious
children. The ones who withheld,

thin-lipped. The most articulate,
sensitive souls suddenly bumbled,
tongue-tied, unable to say anything at all

but the weakest thing, the things that
actually made everything worse.
We're so scared for you. We're so sad for you.

As if our new child had died. I remembered
so vividly the ecstatic leaps of joy
I'd made without condition,

when their children were born. I knew
from several occasions that the most basic
thing to say was: *Congratulations!*

Because our beautiful baby boy
was in fact alive. I heard mostly silence
from the parents of those kids I'd celebrated.

Why on earth would it be the closest,
dearest friends to shit the most toxically
on a sad new family struggling to find

blessing where blessings were?
I wondered. It seemed to me that those
with children could ill afford

to sympathize—we were their nightmares—
how could they not be half-glad
it happened to us and not to them,

our misfortune statistically
tweaking the odds of misfortune
in their favor.

But the guilt of that relief
showed on their faces. A sight
I'll never forget.

Of course, our crisis doesn't actually
mean anything for the likelihood
of others'. It's all a trick

on the parent-heart, and we all fall for it,
how else to sleep? When I was advising
a dear student about her chances

of becoming a Rhodes scholar,
there were many grueling numbers
and pairs of numbers meant to terrify:

forty thousand applicants for twenty-four scholarships,
for example. But once she was a finalist,
I told her: your odds are now 50:50.

Not 852:1. Either you get it or you don't.
Yes, parents. I wish that my son's pain
meant your child would be spared,

but my son is not Christ. And I am no
damn Pietà Mary. In spite of our proximity,
your kid is just as likely to be next. 50:50.

By the way, the student didn't end up
a Rhodes scholar, and I told her
that, for a poet, the experience

of not winning the prize was going to be
more useful than anything else
thus far. Oh, but paltry *usefulness!*

The uses of disappointment are shit
when you just want the big damn prize
or want your child to be able to move

his limbs and talk. Back to the friends,
though, since this is the only place
I can go back to them, it seemed

to me that those most frightened
not only for their children but about
their places in the world, they were the most

grindingly inept, the least able to drum up
compassion. Those gunning for tenure
with little achievement to support it,

stay-at-home moms who had once
been talented but were now pretending
they were not in order to "raise a family"

and to slide into inanity. I don't know what to
make of such spiritual inertia but it seems
like the same stuff racism's made of:

fear of difference: *As long as it's not me,*
I don't have to know anything about it.
As long as they stay the hell away from me,

it never has to be me. As long as they stay
weak enough they can believe they will never
be gutted by this particular pain. *Not my*

child, hurt like that. As long as they seem
incapable of handling such trauma,
God will never force them to.

Secret, smug believers! *God never gives you*
more than you can bear, they like to say, as if
the strong should be punished for their strength:

We can bear it. So we got it.
But what about my baby? How weak does
a newborn have to be to escape God's burdens?

And why press down so hard on Cal when
it was I who grossly claimed superhuman strength:
I know I can deliver him, I know I can

push. I don't care how much pain I'm in,
I can handle it! I can do it! I'm the strongest
fucking woman in the world!

When in fact, if I had let myself be weak,
a C-section would have kept Cal safe
and I'd never have seen the true spirit

of some of my once-close friends.
It's like that old college saying:
Alcohol kills brain cells, but only the weak ones.

I'm certain that I'm merely, unadmirably,
jealous of these friends who certainly
have their own problems,

just not the problem of an injured child,
and I have an uncomfortable,
oozing rage, as if I'd pissed myself

and had to sit in it. Rage that those
who are so fearful of my pain are the ones
who will be most spared it in their own lives.

Let them be poor, then, let them continue
their sexless marriages! Give them
a number of "scares" after which

everything will be fine. A surgery or two.
Misery. Even give them the illnesses
and deaths of their own worthless

parents. These are the mute friends
whose children will be spared.
May they suffer every other misfortune!

I probably shouldn't be telling you
such ugly, monstrous things, Cal,
and I'm not. I'm telling the Andromedans,

to plea for a place in their galaxy.
I want to tell them *I am among weak
people here, and I am strong,*

*and I don't want to be strong anymore.
Let me be weak in your world,
among kind people who are not afraid.*

We'll just have to convince them
that we belong there, Cal, though I'm worried.
I've become bitter and angry,

not at all the kind of citizen I imagine
they'd honor with a new beginning.
But then, "beginning" begins with "beg."

•

Okay, the truth?

I've been wrong or I've been lying
or I've been ignorant. It doesn't matter
which. But now it's time to give it up.

You came from Andromeda, Cal,
that other galaxy. Came to me, to us,
the moment you were born,

when the membrane between
worlds snapped and all that alien love
flooded my body. It came from you.

There was awful confusion because
you didn't seem to be of this world
and the ordinary humans

didn't know what to do. Not even me.
Mommy and her stories, those fairy
tales we have here,

wretched and unending, children
lost in the woods. No wonder you've
always looked at me so quizzically,

a story like that is too tiny to contain
Andromedan you, lost in the Milky Way,
magical boy weak from his first

intergalactic journey to my arms.
I found you, didn't I? I am here.
We found each other, we are here.

And here is where we belong, for here
is where you are you. Exactly you.
Not some other boy in some other world.

I was wrong to mourn so, *he deserves*
better and so forth. You are better.
Better than any lesser truth I could invent.

I opened my eyes from that long dream
to find you here, my perfect child.
You taught me the truth, Cal.

Accept the truth from whoever gives it,
the ancients said to your people.
The truth is you are the truth,

a child born to a liar who is learning
to change. A dashing boy who may never
walk who traveled so far

to be here. A joyful boy who may never
talk who ruthlessly teaches
the teacher the truth

about where children really live.
Where you are alive. You are the most
perfect Calvin Makoto Teicher

of the Universe, a tough, funny
beauty of a boy who holds my hand
and blinks his eyes until I'm

excruciated, mad with love.
How hard it was for you to convince
me that I deserved that love.

My glorious son! A mother's boast
is never merely delusion. A mother
knows, if she can forgive herself

for not knowing. I know now, Cal.
Your frail arms are perfect arms.
Your uncertain eyes, perfect eyes.

Your anguish, your illness, your pain.
Your difficulty, your discovery. Your joy
is my joy and it is a perfect, boundless joy.

God must exist, a God for me after all,
and he must be good, everlastingly so,
to have given you to me.

I don't need any more proof than this.
You in my arms, your little searching fingers
on my face. Wistful, graceful

stars on a wet, clear night.
Galaxies exploding everywhere
around us, exploding in us,

Cal, faster than the lightest light,
so much faster than love,
and our Andromeda, that dream,

I can feel it living in us like *we*
are *its* home. Like it remembers us
from its own childhood.

Oh, maybe, Cal, we *are* home,
if God will let us live here,
with Andromeda inside us,

doesn't it seem we belong?
Now and then, will you help me belong
here, in this place where you became

my child, and I your mother
out of some instant of mystery
of crash and matter

scattered through the cosmos,
God-scooped and poured toward
our bodies. With so much love,

somehow. I am so tired
I cannot beat my own heart anymore.
Cal, shall we stay? Oh let's stay.

We've only just arrived here,
rightly, whirling and weeping,
freely, breathing, brightly born.

ACKNOWLEDGMENTS

I wish to thank the editors of the following magazines: *The Awl,*
Harper's, The Nation, The New Yorker, The Paris Review, Poetry,
The Rumpus, Slate, and *WSQ* (*Women's Studies Quarterly*).

Enormous thanks to the MacDowell Colony, for exquisite
hospitality, beauty, magic. And gratitude to the Corporation
of Yaddo, for generosity, time, space. This book wouldn't exist
without residencies in both places, and was in large part written in
MacDowell's New Jersey and Barnard studios and in Yaddo's West
House. Much work was accomplished thanks to the George A. and
Eliza Gardner Howard Foundation at Brown University. Thank
you, American Academy of Arts and Letters and the Academy of
American Poets.

And with personal gratitude:

To Deborah Landau, Paul Muldoon, Hilton Als, Meghan
O'Rourke and the Pretendettes, Marie Howe, Mark Doty, James
Richardson, Susan Wheeler, J.D. McClatchy, Jayne Anne Phillips,
Alice Elliott Dark, and Rebecca Horne.

To Ann Hood, whose work and compassionate conversation
gave me the courage to write the title poem. (Though she didn't
realize it and therefore shouldn't be held responsible for its
failures.)

This book is especially indebted to the beloved Members of
Team Cal: Sami Akbari, Imelda Laborce, the Roosevelt School,
Yusuke Namiki, Dr. Joseph Levy, Dr. Elizabeth Fiorino, Huck Ho,
Tami Gaines, Robyn Uslip, Lindsay Orcutt, Lauren Joyce, and my
family. And to the special moms who have really been there: Molly
Peryer, Leonie Lewis, Eliza Factor, Aine Carroll, and Jamie Mirabella.

To Dr. Andrew S. Gardner, for Simone.

To Craig. I just love being with you. Even here, on the
acknowledgments page, I am glad to be talking to you. You make
me happy, and you make our kids happy. That's all the kinds of
happiness I need in this life, my love.

ABOUT THE AUTHOR

Brenda Shaughnessy was born in Okinawa, Japan, and grew up in Southern California. She is the author of *Human Dark with Sugar* (Copper Canyon Press, 2008), winner of the James Laughlin Award and finalist for the National Book Critics Circle Award, and *Interior with Sudden Joy* (FSG, 1999). Shaughnessy's poems have appeared in *Best American Poetry, Harper's, The Nation, The New Yorker, The Paris Review,* and *The Rumpus.* She is an assistant professor of English at Rutgers University, Newark, and lives in Brooklyn with her husband, son, and daughter.

Since 1972, Copper Canyon Press has fostered the work of emerging, established, and world-renowned poets for an expanding audience. The Press thrives with the generous patronage of readers, writers, booksellers, librarians, teachers, students, and funders—everyone who shares the belief that poetry is vital to language and living.

MAJOR SUPPORT HAS BEEN PROVIDED BY:

THE PAUL G. ALLEN
FAMILY FOUNDATION

THE MAURER FAMILY
FOUNDATION

NATIONAL
ENDOWMENT
FOR THE ARTS

WASHINGTON STATE
ARTS COMMISSION

The Paul G. Allen Family Foundation

Amazon.com

Anonymous

Arcadia Fund

John Branch

Diana and Jay Broze

Beroz Ferrell & The Point, LLC

Mimi Gardner Gates

Golden Lasso, LLC

Gull Industries, Inc.
on behalf of William and Ruth True

Carolyn and Robert Hedin

Lannan Foundation

Rhoady and Jeanne Marie Lee

The Maurer Family Foundation

National Endowment for the Arts

New Mexico Community Foundation

Penny and Jerry Peabody

Joseph C. Roberts

Cynthia Lovelace Sears and Frank Buxton

Washington State Arts Commission

Charles and Barbara Wright

To learn more about underwriting Copper Canyon Press titles,
please call 360-385-4925 ext. 103

The poems are set in Sabon. The display type is Sackers Gothic Medium.
Book design and composition by Phil Kovacevich.
Printed on archival-quality paper at McNaughton & Gunn, Inc.

The Chinese character for poetry is made up of two parts:
"word" and "temple." It also serves as pressmark for
Copper Canyon Press.